spirelli®

Jane Hermsen

FORTE PUBLISHERS

Contents

ISBN 90 5877 271 3

This is a publication from
Forte Publishers BV
P.O. Box 1394
3500 BJ Utrecht
The Netherlands

For more information about the creative books available from Forte Uitgevers:
www.hobby-party.com

Publisher: Marianne Perlot
Editor: Hanny Vlaar
Photography and digital image editing:
Fotografie Gerhard Witteveen,
Apeldoorn, the Netherlands
Cover and inner design:
Studio Herman Bade BV, Baarn,
the Netherlands
Translation:
TextCase, Groningen, the Netherlands

Preface

Whilst doing the photography work for the **Mosaic Punching** and **Paper Weaving books**, I was asked to do something with Spirelli cards and thread. And of course, I always want to try something new. Once I got home, I couldn't wait to see what could be done and I spent several hours finding out. Even my children wanted to help. I found it to be addictive, so be careful. Winding attractive thread around the cards gives a wonderful result each and every time.

Good luck with the cards.

Jane

Thanks

Marc for helping to wind the thread on the cards, Lisette for her help with the computer when I didn't know what to do and everybody who has helped to make this book.

Techniques

Spirelli cards

The Spirelli cards can be bought in a number of different colours. An oval and a circle have been punched on every card, so that you only need to press them out. You can use the card which is left over as a frame.

The winding

Stick a metallic thread to the back of the Spirelli card using a piece of adhesive tape. Start with one of the points and wind the thread around the card. Skip, for example, nine points and continue winding the thread around the card using the next point. Always wind the thread around the Spirelli card at an angle and from the front to the back. Wind the thread all the way around the Spirelli card. When you are finished, cut the thread off and stick it to the back of the card using adhesive tape. The more points you skip, the smaller the opening in the middle. If you skip fewer points, the opening in the middle will be larger. In this way, you can alter the size of the opening to the size of the picture you wish to stick in the middle.

Metallic thread

Attractive, shiny thread by Madeira is available in many different colours.

Sticker sheets

Use all kinds of borders and edges from sticker sheets to decorate the cards. Often, really nice pieces are left on the sticker sheets which you can also use these to decorate the Spirelli cards. Stick gold or silver dots on the points.

Tip

Do you have a lot of reels of thread? Then take a piece of wood (4 x 4 x 40 cm) and hammer a nail into it every 4 cm, so that they protrude 2 cm. If you put the reels on the nails, they will not roll off of the table.

First thread

Second thread

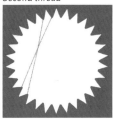

Skipping 8 points

Skipping 12 points

1. Materials

2. Wind the thread around the Spirelli card

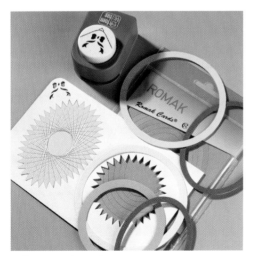

3. Frames and punches

4. Decorate with stickers

Materials

- ❑ Cards with matching envelopes (Romak)
- ❑ Spirelli cards
- ❑ Zigzag cards (Romak)
- ❑ Flower cards (Romak)
- ❑ Frames (Romak)
- ❑ Metallic thread (Madeira)
- ❑ Sticker sheets

- ❑ Mini 3D cutting sheets:
  AM 1001 (Christmas),
  AM 1002 (Animals),
  AM 1003 (Baby),
  AM 1004 (Spring)
- ❑ Organza ribbon
- ❑ Photo glue
- ❑ Corner and border punches

- ❑ Transparent ruler with a metal cutting edge (Securit)
- ❑ 3D scissors
- ❑ Foam tape
- ❑ Cutting mat and knife

Specific materials are given at the start of each chapter.

Cards on the cover and page 1

Butterflies

Take a yellow, square zigzag card. Cut a square (9 x 9 cm) out of dark blue card and stick it in the card so that 0.5 cm of dark blue card is visible around the square of the zigzag card. Stick a dark blue Spirelli card on the card. Wind gold thread around a yellow Spirelli card, skipping 9 points. Stick the yellow card on the dark blue card, making sure all the points are visible. Cut out all the pictures. Stick the butterflies in the top left-hand corner using foam tape. Stick the basket of flowers in the middle of the Spirelli card and the other pictures on the right-hand side of the card. Decorate the card with a decorative border and sticker dots.

50

Start with a light blue card (12.5 x 12.5 cm) with a round opening. Stick the outer frame of a set of gold, round frames on the card. Stick a gold thread between the small gold frame and the card to hang the Spirelli card on.
Wind gold thread around a light blue Spirelli card, skipping 8 points. Stick this on a white Spirelli card, with the gold thread between the two.
Make sure all the points are visible. Decorate the top Spirelli card with sticker dots and let it hang in the card.

Spring

Spring is when you start spending time in the garden.

What you need
- ❏ Card: yellow (no. 67), white (no. 21) and light blue (no. 28)
- ❏ Spirelli cards of the same colour
- ❏ Mini 3D cutting sheet (AM 1004)
- ❏ Metallic thread: yellow and blue
- ❏ Corner and border punches
- ❏ Sticker sheets

All the cards measure 12.5 x 12.5 cm.

1. Mouse

Take a light blue card. Cut a strip (7.4 x 11.4 cm) from a yellow Spirelli frame. Punch a border in the top and bottom and stick the frame on the card. Wind blue metallic thread around a light blue Spirelli card, skipping 9 points. Cut out the mouse and the broom and stick them on the card using foam tape. Also cut out the butterfly and the birdhouse and stick them on the card using glue. Wind metallic thread around the card and tie it together on the inside of the card.

2. Duck

Take a yellow card. Cut a strip (8 x 12.5 cm) from a white Spirelli frame. Use a border punch to punch an attractive border in this strip and stick it on the card. Wind pale yellow metallic thread around a yellow Spirelli card, skipping 9 points. Stick the card inside the frame. Stick the small duck in the middle of the Spirelli card using foam tape. Wind a thread around the card and tie it together on the inside of the card.

3. Frog

Take a yellow card. Cut a strip (8.2 x 12.5 cm) from a white Spirelli frame. Punch out the corners and stick the strip on the card. Wind yellow thread around a yellow Spirelli card, skipping 8 points. Stick it in the white frame. Cut out the pictures and stick them on the card using foam tape. Stick the chickens on the card, alternating between foam tape and glue.

4. Flower basket

Take a light blue card. Cut a strip (7.4 x 11.4 cm) from a yellow Spirelli frame. Punch an attractive pattern in the corners using a corner punch. Wind blue metallic thread around a light blue Spirelli card, skipping 9 points. Stick the yellow Spirelli frame on the card and stick the light blue Spirelli card in this. Cut out a basket of flowers and stick it on the card using foam tape. Finally, wind a blue thread around the card.

1.

2.

3.

4.

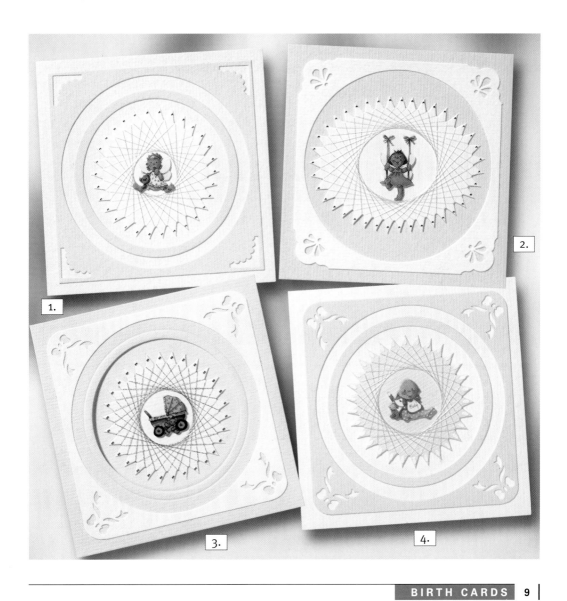

1.

2.

3.

4.

Birth cards

Has somebody given birth?
Then send a pale yellow card
and you can't go wrong.

What you need
- ❏ *Card: white (21),*
  ivory (22) and
  yellow (67)
- ❏ *Spirelli cards of the same colour*
- ❏ *Round frames:*
  yellow and white
- ❏ *Mini 3D cutting sheet*
  (AM 1003)
- ❏ *Metallic thread:*
  yellow and blended pastel
- ❏ *Corner punches*
- ❏ *Sticker sheets: gold and white*

All the cards measure 12.5 x 12.5 cm.

1. Elf

Take an ivory card. Stick the outer frame from a set of round frames on the card, but punch out the corners first using a corner punch. Take a frame that is two sizes smaller than the outer frame and stick it on the card. Wind pale yellow thread around a white Spirelli card, skipping 11 points. Cut out the elf and stick it on the card using foam tape. Decorate the card with dots from a gold sticker sheet.

2. On the swing

Take a yellow card. Stick the outer frame from a set of white, round frames on the card, but punch out the corners first. Wind pale yellow thread around a white, oval Spirelli card, skipping 13 points. Cut out the elf on the swing and stick it on the card using foam tape. Finally, add sticker dots to all the points of the oval Spirelli card.

3. Pram

Take a yellow card with a round opening. Stick the outer frame from a set of white, round frames on the card and punch out the corners using a corner punch. Wind blended pastel thread around an ivory Spirelli card, skipping 10 points. Stick everything together. Cut out a pram and stick it on the card using foam tape. Decorate the card with dots from a sticker sheet.

4. Baby with a cat

Take a white card. Stick the outer frame from a set of round frames on this card, but first punch out the corners using a corner punch. Also stick the second largest yellow frame on the card. Wind pale yellow thread around a yellow Spirelli card, skipping 9 points. Cut out the baby with the cat and stick them in the middle using foam tape. Decorate the points with white dots from a sticker sheet.

Cute cards

Are you moving in with somebody or starting a family? Then send everybody a nice card with birds and rabbits.

What you need
- ❏ *Card: white (no. 21), light blue (no. 28), salmon (no. 64) and mint (no. 65)*
- ❏ *Spirelli cards of the same colour*
- ❏ *Flower cards: white, light blue and mint*
- ❏ *Mini 3D cutting sheet (AM 1003)*
- ❏ *Metallic thread: white, light blue and light green*
- ❏ *Organza ribbon and narrow ribbon*
- ❏ *Corner punches*

All the square cards measure 12.5 x 12.5 cm. For the rectangular cards, fold a card (10.5 x 29.6 cm) double.

1. Baby Blue
Make a light blue card and stick a white flower card on it. Punch two holes in the fold of the card. Thread a blue Organza ribbon through the holes and tie it into an attractive bow. Wind white metallic thread around a light blue Spirelli card, skipping 9 points. Cut out the baby and stick it in the middle of the Spirelli card using foam tape.

2. Birds
Make a white card and punch two holes in the fold. Thread a blue Organza ribbon through the holes and tie it into an attractive bow. Stick a light blue flower card on the card. Wind blue metallic thread around a white Spirelli card, skipping 11 points. Cut out the love birds and stick them in the middle of the Spirelli card.

3. Salmon
Punch out the top and bottom right-hand corners of a salmon card. Stick a white flower card on the card. Wind white metallic thread around a salmon Spirelli card, skipping 10 points. Cut out the baby and stick it in the middle of the Spirelli card using foam tape. Finally, wind a salmon ribbon around the card.

4. Bear
Punch a pretty pattern in two corners of a white card. Stick a mint green flower card on the card. Wind light green thread around a white Spirelli card, skipping 9 points. Make two holes in the fold and thread a mint green ribbon through them. Cut out the bear and stick it in the middle of the Spirelli card using foam tape.

5. Rabbits
Punch out two corners of a mint green card. Stick a white flower card on the card. Wind light green thread around a mint green Spirelli card, skipping 10 points. Cut out the rabbits and stick them in the middle of the Spirelli card. Finally, wind a mint green ribbon around the card.

1.

2.

3.

4.

5.

Elves and angels

These elves and angels wish

you a merry Christmas.

What you need
- ❏ *Card: white (no. 21) and*
  light blue (no. 28)
- ❏ *Spirelli cards of the same colour*
- ❏ *Erica's vellum*
  (Christmas white and gold)
- ❏ *Mini 3D cutting sheets:*
  AM 1001 and AM 1003
- ❏ *Metallic thread: silver and gold*
- ❏ *Sticker sheets: silver and gold*
- ❏ *Text sticker*

All the cards measure 12.5 x 12.5 cm. Decorate the cards with sticker dots and decorative borders. Stick the pictures on the cards using foam tape.

How to stick the vellum on the card
Stick a piece of double-sided adhesive tape to the back of the card along the fold. Fold the vellum double and slide it over the card.

1. Angel with a lantern
Take a light blue card. Cut a strip (12.5 x 21 cm) from a piece of vellum with white stars. Fold it double and stick it on the card. Wind silver thread around a light blue, oval Spirelli card, skipping 14 points. Stick the angel in the middle of the Spirelli card.

2. White angel
Take a white card. Cut a strip (12.5 x 21 cm) from a piece of vellum with gold stars. Fold it double and stick it on the card. Wind gold thread around a white, oval Spirelli card, skipping 12 points. Stick a white angel in the middle of the Spirelli card.

3. Elf with stars
Take a light blue card. Cut a strip (12.5 x 21 cm) from a piece of vellum with gold Christmas trees. Fold it double and stick it on the card. Wind gold thread around a white, oval Spirelli card, skipping 12 points. Stick the elf in the middle of the Spirelli card.

4. Angel with a trumpet
Take a white card. Cut a strip (12.5 x 21 cm) from a piece of vellum with white stars. Fold it double and stick it on the card. Wind silver thread around a white, oval Spirelli card, skipping 14 points. Stick the angel in the middle of the Spirelli card.

5. Christmas baby
Take a light blue card. Cut a strip (21 x 12.5 cm) from a piece of vellum with white stars. Fold it double and stick it on the card. Wind silver thread around a light blue, oval Spirelli card, skipping 8 points. Stick the elf in the middle of the Spirelli card.

Seasons greetings

Attractive Christmas cards
made from printed vellum
and Organza ribbon.

What you need
- ❏ *Card: white (no. 21), green (no. 24) and*
  aubergine (no. 26)
- ❏ *Spirelli cards: white, aubergine, green and sand*
- ❏ *Printed vellum in different colours*
- ❏ *Mini 3D cutting sheet (AM 1001)*
- ❏ *Organza ribbon in different colours*
- ❏ *Metallic thread: gold*
- ❏ *Sticker sheets: gold*

All the square cards measure 12.5 x 12.5 cm.

See page 14 for instructions on how to stick the vellum to the card.

1. White and gold
Take a white card (10.5 x 14.5 cm). Cut a strip of printed vellum to the same size as the card, fold it double and stick it on the card. Wind gold Organza ribbon around the card and stick it on the front of the card where the Spirelli card is going to be positioned using double-sided adhesive tape. Wind gold thread around a sand-coloured Spirelli card, skipping 16 points. Stick the card on the ribbon. Make a separate bow from Organza ribbon and stick it at the top of the Spirelli card. Finally, decorate the points with dots from a sticker sheet.

2. Two candles
Take a square aubergine card. Cut a strip (12.5 x 21 cm) from dark red printed vellum, fold it double and stick it on the card. Wind gold thread around a sand-coloured Spirelli card, skipping 11 points. Stick the Spirelli card on the card using double-sided adhesive tape. Cut out two candles in pots and stick them in the middle of the Spirelli card. Decorate the points with gold dots from a sticker sheet.

Make two holes in the fold of the card. Thread a gold Organza ribbon through the holes and tie it into a pretty bow.

3. Christmas green

Take a green card. Cut a strip (12.5 x 21 cm) from white printed vellum, fold it double and stick it on the card. Wind gold thread around a green Spirelli card, skipping 11 points. Stick a suitable picture in the middle of the Spirelli card and decorate the points with dots from a sticker sheet. Make two holes in the fold of the card. Thread a green Organza ribbon through the holes and tie it into a pretty bow.

4. Aubergine with white

Take a white card. Cut a strip (12.5 x 21 cm) from dark red printed vellum, fold it double and stick it on the card. Wind gold Organza ribbon lengthways around the card. Stick the ribbon to the front of the card where the Spirelli card will be located using double-sided adhesive tape. Wind gold thread around an aubergine Spirelli card, skipping 12 points. Stick the card on the ribbon. Make a separate bow from Organza ribbon and stick it at the top of the Spirelli card. Decorate the points with sticker dots and stick a decorative border on the side of the card.

5. Christmas red and Christmas green

Take a green card. Cut a strip (12.5 x 21 cm) from red printed vellum, fold it double and stick it on the card.

Wind gold thread around a green Spirelli card, skipping 12 points. Cut out a picture with berries and stick it in the middle of the Spirelli card using foam tape. Decorate the points with gold sticker dots. Make two holes in the fold of the card. Thread a red Organza ribbon through the holes and tie it into a pretty bow.

6. Blue

Take a white card. Cut a strip (12.5 x 21 cm) from blue/red printed vellum, fold it double and stick it on the card. Wind gold thread around a white Spirelli card, skipping 11 points. Make two holes in the fold of the card. Thread a white Organza ribbon through the holes and tie it into a pretty bow. Cut out two candles and stick them in the middle of the Spirelli card using foam tape. Decorate the card with dots and a decorative border from a sticker sheet.

Polar animals

Baby animals are just as soft as new-born babies. That's why they make such a good combination.

What you need
- ❏ *Card: white (no. 21), light blue (no. 28) and lilac (no. 69)*
- ❏ *Spirelli cards: white and light blue*
- ❏ *Vellum: Perkaline white (Papicolor)*
- ❏ *Mini 3D cutting sheet (AM 1002)*
- ❏ *Ribbon: blue and pink*
- ❏ *Metallic thread: blue, white and pink*
- ❏ *Text stickers: silver*

Cards with a ribbon
For the rectangular cards with a ribbon, fold a strip of card (10.5 x 29.6 cm) double and make two holes in the fold. Thread a ribbon through the holes and tie it into a pretty bow. Decorate the cards with a text sticker.

Spirelli frame
Use the leftovers of the Spirelli cards as frames on the cards.

1. Penguin
Take a light blue card. Wind light blue metallic thread around a light blue Spirelli card, skipping 10 points.

Cut a strip (7 x 10.5 cm) from a white Spirelli frame and stick it on the card. Stick four penguins on the card using foam tape.

2. Seals
Take a white card. Make two half Spirelli frames (one lilac and one light blue), each measuring 3.5 x 10.5 cm, and carefully stick them together on the white card. Wind light blue metallic thread around a white Spirelli card, skipping 11 points. Stick the Spirelli card exactly in the two-coloured frame. Stick the large seal on the card using foam tape and stick the small seal on the card using glue.

3. Afternoon nap

Make a double card (10.5 x 14.8 cm) from white card and white vellum. Stick them together by sticking double-sided adhesive tape on the back of the card against the fold. Draw a thin pencil line 1 cm from the bottom of the vellum and cut along the line using a pair of figure scissors. Rub out any of the pencil line which remains. Wind silver thread around a white Spirelli card, skipping 11 points. Stick this and a light blue Spirelli card on the card. Stick the sleeping polar bear on the card using foam tape.

4. Mother and child

Take a white card. Wind pink metallic thread around a white Spirelli card, skipping 10 points. Cut a strip (7.7 x 10.5 cm) from a lilac Spirelli frame and stick it on the card. Cut out the baby polar bear and stick it in the middle of the Spirelli card using foam tape. Stick the mother polar bear with the baby bear on the card using foam tape.

5. Baby polar bear

Take a light blue card. Wind pink metallic thread around a light blue Spirelli card. Make two half Spirelli frames (one lilac and one light blue) and carefully stick them together with the Spirelli card in the middle. Stick the baby polar bears on the card using foam tape.

Merry Christmas

Decorate your Christmas tree in lilac and aubergine and make these Christmas cards to match.

What you need
- ❏ *Zigzag cards (12.5 x 12.5 cm): white (no. 21), aubergine (no. 26) and lilac (no. 69)*
- ❏ *Card: white and lilac*
- ❏ *Spirelli cards of the same colour*
- ❏ *Mini 3D cutting sheet (AM 1001)*
- ❏ *Ribbon: silver*
- ❏ *Metallic thread: silver*
- ❏ *Sticker sheets: silver*

Zigzag cards

Stick a square (9 x 9 cm) of a matching colour inside the card so that when the card has been folded closed 0.5 cm remains visible on three sides of the zigzag part of the card.

Two Spirelli cards in different colours are stuck on top of each other on the zigzag cards so that all the points remain visible.

Card on page 3

Take a square aubergine card (12.5 x 12.5 cm). Cut a strip (7.9 x 12.5 cm) from a lilac Spirelli frame and stick it on the aubergine card. Wind silver thread around an aubergine Spirelli card, skipping 12 points.

Stick this on the Spirelli frame, so that the points of the frame and the Spirelli card are visible. It will look just like a decoration for a Christmas tree. Stick a ribbon or a strip from a sticker sheet above the Spirelli Christmas ball. Decorate the card with a ribbon and stick a strip from a sticker sheet along both sides. Stick the pictures on the card using foam tape. Decorate the points of the Spirelli card with dots from a sticker sheet.

1. Red apples

Take an aubergine zigzag card. Cut out a square from lilac card and stick it in the zigzag card. Stick a lilac Spirelli card on the zigzag card. Wind silver thread around a white Spirelli card, skipping 11 points. Cut out the pictures and hang the lanterns from a strip from a sticker sheet. Decorate the card with a decorative border and stick dots from a silver sticker sheet on the white points. Stick the other pictures on the card using foam tape.

2. Merry Christmas

Take a white zigzag card. Cut out a square from aubergine card and stick it in the zigzag card. Stick a lilac Spirelli card on the zigzag card. Wind silver thread around an aubergine Spirelli card, skipping 13 points. Stick silver dots from a sticker sheet on the lilac points. Make sure all the points are visible. Decorate the card with decorative borders from a sticker sheet. Cut out the pictures. Stick the bear in the bottom left-hand corner and the two candles in pots in the bottom right-hand corner. Finally, stick a ribbon on the Spirelli Christmas decoration.

3. Poinsettia

Take a white zigzag card. Cut out a square from aubergine card and stick it in the zigzag card. Stick an aubergine Spirelli card on the zigzag card and decorate the points with dots from a sticker sheet. Wind silver thread around a lilac Spirelli card, skipping 8 points. Cut out the Christmas ball and the pot with the poinsettia. Stick them on the card using foam tape and hang the Christmas balls from a silver strip. Stick the poinsettia in the bottom right-hand corner.

4. Lilac Christmas

Take a lilac zigzag card. Cut out a square from aubergine card and stick it in the zigzag card. Cut out some small Christmas pictures and stick them around the zigzag frame using foam tape. Decorate the card with a border from a sticker sheet. Stick an aubergine Spirelli card on the square of the zigzag card. Wind silver thread around a white Spirelli card, skipping 10 points. Stick a dot from a sticker sheet on every white point. Hang the Spirelli Christmas ball on a silver strip and decorate it with a ribbon.

Adorable animals

I'm sure you know somebody who you can make happy with one of these animal cards.

What you need
- ❏ *Zigzag cards: ivory (no. 22), dark blue (no. 25), mint (no. 65), sand (no. 66) and yellow (no. 67)*
- ❏ *Card: green (no. 24), salmon (no. 64), ivory (no. 22), light blue (no. 28) and sand (no. 66)*
- ❏ *Spirelli cards in matching colours*
- ❏ *Mini 3D cutting sheets: AM 1002 and AM 1004*
- ❏ *Metallic thread: white and reddish brown*
- ❏ *Sticker sheets: silver and gold*

Zigzag cards
Stick a square (9 x 9 cm) in the card so that 0.5 cm remains visible on three sides of the zigzag part of the card. Stick a Spirelli card of the same colour on the square and stick an adhesive border around it. The points of the bottom and top Spirelli cards must remain visible.

1. Squirrels
Take a sand card. The square and the bottom Spirelli card are ivory. Wind reddish brown thread around a sand-coloured Spirelli card, skipping 7 points. Stick the pictures on the card using foam tape.

2. Piglets
Take an ivory card. The square and the bottom Spirelli card are salmon coloured. Wind white metallic thread around an ivory Spirelli card, skipping 11 points. Stick the piglets on the card using foam tape.

3. Green frog card
Take a light green card. The square and the bottom Spirelli card are dark green. Wind white metallic thread around a mint green Spirelli card, skipping 10 points. Stick a butterfly in the middle of the Spirelli card using glue and stick the other pictures on the card using foam tape.

4. Blue frog card
Take a blue card. The square and the bottom Spirelli card are light blue. Wind white metallic thread around a dark blue Spirelli card, skipping 10 points. Stick one butterfly in the middle of the Spirelli card using glue and stick the other pictures on the card using foam tape.

5. Kittens
Take a yellow card. The square and the bottom Spirelli card are sand coloured. Wind white metallic thread around a yellow Spirelli card, skipping 10 points. Stick four kittens and the bowl on the card using foam tape.

Numbers and letters

A stylish card with the right number or a monogram for the person receiving the card.

What you need
- ❏ Card: white (no. 21), light blue (no. 28), salmon (no. 64), mint (no. 65) and lilac (no. 69)
- ❏ Spirelli cards: white, salmon, light blue, lilac, aubergine and mint
- ❏ Round frames: white, yellow and lilac
- ❏ Flower card: white
- ❏ Perkaline vellum: blue, green and salmon (Papicolor)
- ❏ Metallic thread: silver, gold, blue and pink
- ❏ Line border punch (Diamond)
- ❏ Sticker sheets with numbers and letters

1. Salmon
Take a salmon card (10.5 x 14.8 cm). Cut a strip (14.8 x 21 cm) from orange vellum and fold it double. Punch an attractive border along one side of the vellum using the Line border punch. Stick a strip of double-sided adhesive tape on the back of the salmon card, next to the fold, and stick the vellum to the tape. Wind silver thread around a salmon Spirelli card, skipping 12 points. Stick a white Spirelli card on the orange vellum and stick the salmon Spirelli card on top of that. Make sure the white points remain visible. Stick a monogram in the middle of the Spirelli card and decorate the card with dots from a sticker sheet.

2. 12,5
Take an ivory card (12.5 x 12.5 cm) with a round opening. Take the outer frame from a set of yellow, round frames and punch out the corners. Stick the frame on the card. Stick a yellow Spirelli card in the card. Wind gold, shiny thread around an ivory Spirelli card, skipping 12 points. Stick the Spirelli card in the card, making sure the yellow points remain visible. Decorate the cards with suitable numbers.

3. M & A
Cut a 10 cm long strip from an A4 card. This card fits exactly in a bank envelope. Fold the light blue card double Do the same to a sheet of blue vellum. Use the Line border punch to punch out the border of the vellum. Stick the card and the vellum together (see the instructions given for card 1). Wind light blue thread around two light blue Spirelli cards, skipping 11 points. Stick them on the blue vellum and decorate the card with the correct monograms.

4. Silver anniversary
Take a white card (12.5 x 12.5 cm) with a round opening. Take the outer frame from a set of lilac, round borders and punch out all the corners.

Stick this on the white card. Stick a lilac Spirelli card in the card. Wind gold thread around an aubergine Spirelli card, skipping 11 points.

Stick a dot on every point and stick a number from a gold sticker sheet in the middle of the Spirelli card.

5. Many thanks

Take a mint green card (12.5 x 12.5 cm). Cut a strip (12.5 x 20 cm) from green vellum and fold it double. Use the Line border punch to punch a decorative border in the vellum. Stick both cards together according to the instructions given for card 1. Stick a white Spirelli card on the green vellum. Wind silver thread around a mint green Spirelli card, skipping 12 points.

Stick the mint green Spirelli card on the white Spirelli card, making sure the white points remain visible. Decorate the card with text, a monogram, dots and a silver border.

6. 50

Take a lilac card (12.5 x 12.5 cm) with a round opening. Take the outer frame from a set of white, round borders and punch out the corners. Stick the frame on the card. Stick a white flower card in the card. Stick an aubergine Spirelli card on this card. Wind pink thread around a lilac Spirelli card, skipping 10 points. Stick it on the aubergine Spirelli card, making sure the aubergine points remain visible. Decorate the card with dots and a number from a sticker sheet.

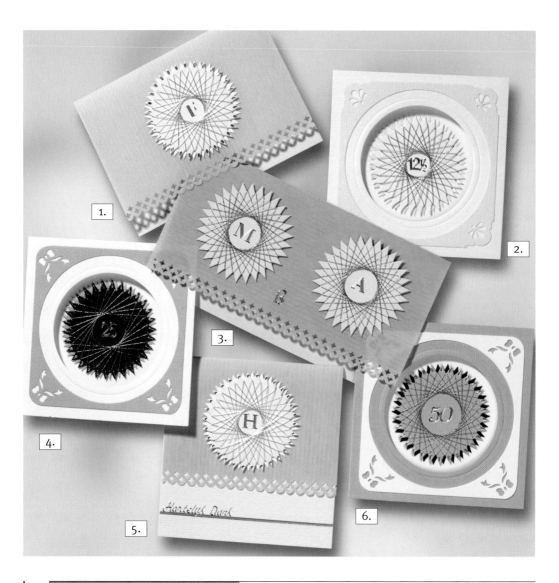

1.

2.

3.

4.

5.

6.

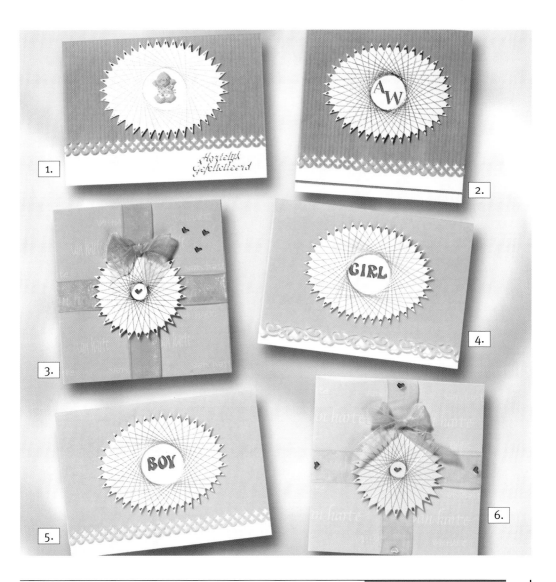

Pastel colours

Vellum looks very nice

on a white card.

What you need
- ❏ Card: light blue (no. 28),
  white (no. 21) and lilac (no. 69)
- ❏ Spirelli cards:
  white and light blue
- ❏ Coloured vellum, with or without text
- ❏ Mini 3D cutting sheet (AM 1003)
- ❏ Organza ribbon: pink and blue
- ❏ Line border punches: diamond and heart
- ❏ Metallic thread: silver, gold, pink, lilac and white
- ❏ Sticker sheets: silver and gold
- ❏ Sticker sheets with letters

These cards measure 12.5 x 12.5 cm or 10.5 x 14.8 cm. Decorate them with stickers.

See page 14 for instructions on how to stick the vellum to the card.

1. Baby
Take a white card. Cut a piece of purple vellum (14.8 x 19.5 cm), fold it double and punch an attractive border in it. Wind white thread around a white Spirelli card, skipping 14 points. Stick the picture in the middle of the Spirelli card using foam tape.

2. Letter card
Take a white card. Cut a piece of purple vellum (12.5 x 22 cm), fold it double and punch an attractive border along one side. Wind pink thread around a white, oval Spirelli card, skipping 15 points. Stick the Spirelli card on the front.

3. Pink card with hearts
Take a lilac card. Fold a piece of pink vellum with text (12.5 x 12.5 cm) around the card. Make a 3 cm long incision in the fold of both cards (this is for the ribbon to pass through). Wind pink thread around a white Spirelli card, skipping 13 points.
Cut two ribbons, each 28 cm long. Fold the ribbons vertically and horizontally around the card (through the incisions in the folds).
Stick these to the front of the card using double-sided adhesive tape and stick the Spirelli card in the middle. Decorate the card with a bow.

4. Girl
Take a white card. Cut a piece of pink vellum (10.5 x 14.8 cm), fold it double and punch an attractive border in one side. Wind silver thread around a white, oval Spirelli card, skipping 14 points.

5. Boy
Follow the instructions given for card 4.

6. Blue card with hearts.
Follow the instructions given for card 3.

Condolences

A home-made condolence card gives something extra during a difficult time.

What you need
- ❏ *Card: white (no. 21),*
  black and grey
- ❏ *Spirelli cards of the same colour*
- ❏ *Oval and square frames:*
  silver and grey
- ❏ *Metallic thread:*
  silver, gold and black
- ❏ *Stickers: silver and gold*

*These cards measure 12.5 x 12.5 cm or 10.5 x 14.8 cm.
Decorate them with stickers.*

Spirelli frame: use leftover Spirelli cards as the frames on the cards.

1. Condolences in silver
Take a grey card. Cut a strip (7.5 x 12.4 cm) from a black Spirelli frame and stick it on the card. Wind silver thread around a white Spirelli card, skipping 8 points. Stick the Spirelli card in the black frame.

2. Take care
Take a white, square card with a square opening. Stick a silver frame around the opening. Wind a silver and black blended thread around a grey Spirelli card, skipping 11 points.

3. Sincere commiserations
Take a white card. Wind gold thread around a black Spirelli card, skipping 10 points. Stick it on the card, slightly above the middle. Stick gold borders on the card and stick a cross in the middle of the Spirelli card.

4. Condolences in gold
Take a white, square card. I have embossed a circle on the white card using a round embossing template. Wind gold thread around a black Spirelli card, skipping 9 points. Stick this on the white card.

5. Condolences in grey
Take a white card and stick the outer frame from a set of grey, oval frames on it. Stick the second largest grey frame on the card. Wind black and gold blended thread around a grey Spirelli card, skipping 12 points.

6. Square card
Take a black, square card. Cut a strip (8.2 x 9.5 cm) from a grey Spirelli frame.
Wind silver thread around a white Spirelli card, skipping 11 points.

Thanks to Romak B.V. in Hillegom, the Netherlands, for supplying the materials.

Shopkeepers can order the materials from Avec. B.V. in Waalwijk, the Netherlands.